Praise for *Arise and Witness*

"These poems, like Anne's life of radical pacifism, seek to unite in concrete ways her love of God, witness to God's people, and love of the earth and creation. May they inspire us all to act on behalf of all three. Her words are even more timely today than when first written… Anne Montgomery… ¡presente!"
—Jackie Allen-Douçot, member of the Hartford Catholic Worker and the Griffiss and Thames River Plowshares.
—Clare Grady, member of the Ithaca Catholic Worker, Griffiss Plowshares and Kings Bay Plowshares 7.

"Publishing this collection of Sr. Anne Montgomery's poetry allows us to call upon her spirit and her wisdom imparting inspiration and hope. Reading and speaking of her artfully braided words enhance the light of her ongoing presence in the Beloved Community. "
—Dean Hammer, member of the Plowshares Eight and Griffiss Plowshares. He practices psychotherapy in Vermont, and teaches clinical psychology at Antioch University New England.

"Just as the sands of time nearly erodes the memory of even closest of friends and experiences and it gets further between photos and anecdotes, along comes a work by Laffin & Sargent to retrieve a concentrated sitting with the friend in her crucible of the courts, plowshares, West Banks & Gaza, and textures of her distillation of her being among us…linger with Sister Anne's advocacy, her quiet fire."
—Steve Kelly, S.J., co-defendant with Sr. Anne Montgomery, Disarm Now Plowshares.

ii

Arise and Witness

Arise and Witness

Poems by Anne Montgomery, RSCJ
About Faith, Prison, War Zones and
Nonviolent Resistance

Edited by Arthur Laffin
with Carole Sargent

NAP NEW ACADEMIA PUBLISHING · SCARITH

Washington, DC

Library of Congress Control Number: 2024909674
ISBN 979-8-9900542-4-0 paperback (alk. paper)

SCARITH   An imprint of New Academia Publishing

New Academia Publishing
4401-A Connecticut Ave. NW, #236, Washington DC 20008
info@newacademia.com - www.newacademia.com

In loving memory of
Anne Montgomery, RSCJ

Contents

Acknowledgements

From Arthur Laffin

During the time of Anne's funeral at the Oakwood Convent of the Sacred Heart in Atherton, California, I was given a folder of her poems by sisters from her Community. I held onto them for a while and, over time, as I would read them, I thought that these poems definitely needed to be shared with a wider readership. Eventually, I conferred with Sr. Clare Pratt, RSCJ, and Carole Sargent, about the possibility of publishing them. Carole and I also communicated with Sr. Diane Roche, RSCJ, Sr. Fran Tobin, RSCJ, and Sr. Lyn Osiek, RSCJ. Everyone consulted expressed their support. Carole enthusiastically offered to contact New Academia Publishing to see if they would do it. After submitting a prospectus, they agreed. Thus, Carole and I began our collaboration on developing this book.

We convey our sincere gratitude to Sisters Clare, Fran, Lyn and the RSCJ Community for their heartfelt support in publishing Anne's poems. We are ever so grateful to New Academia for publishing this volume.

I am immensely grateful to Carole for her exceptional painstaking work on this book from start to finish. Without all her diligent efforts this book simply would not be published.

I want to convey deep gratitude to Sr. Clare Pratt for her preface, to John Schuchardt, Rabbi Lynn Gottlieb, Anna Brown and Dean Hammer for their poignant reflections, and to Jackie Allen-Douçot and Clare Grady for their introduction to Anne's Alderson Lenten prison poem. I also want to thank Lynn for the photo of the mural dedicated to Anne in Hebron, a mural she helped to create.

I want to express special thanks to Paul Magno and Sr. Clare for their special contribution of proofreading the manuscript. And I convey great gratitude to my wife, Colleen McCarthy, and my son,

Carlos, for their support throughout the course of this book project. I also want to convey appreciation to the community of Anne Montgomery House in Washington, DC for the gracious hospitality offered to Carole and I for a meeting we had there in the early stages of our work on this manuscript.

Finally, we thank God for Anne Montgomery, whose exemplary life of Gospel fidelity is the ultimate inspiration for this book. Her poems are the fruit of being a Religious of the Sacred Heart, her relationships with the victims and the poor, and different communities she worked and witnessed with to proclaim God's reign of justice, love, nonviolence and peace. These communities include: the Kairos Community in New York City, the Plowshares Communities she acted with and the extended plowshares movement, Jonah House, the Atlantic Life Community, Southern Life Community, Pacific Life Community, the Christian Peacemaker Teams (now Community Peacemakers Teams), and the Catholic Worker houses she was associated with on the east and west coasts, including the Dorothy Day Catholic Worker in Washington, DC. To these communities and to all the people whom Anne befriended and accompanied, including in prison and war zones--Deo Gratias! Through God's amazing grace, a transcendent communion with Anne, now among the holy cloud of witnesses, continues!

From Carole Sargent

The book is already dedicated to Anne Montgomery, but I additionally "dedicate" this to Carol Gilbert, OP and Jeanne Clark OP, who both keep me cognizant of the role of poetry inspired by nonviolent resistance that so often led to the arrest and incarceration of Catholic sisters. Both of them wrote poetry in jails and prisons, and I helped Sr. Jeanne publish a nonfiction book with Orbis and Robert Ellsberg that featured some of those poems. I am currently working with Sr. Carol Gilbert on a biography of Ardeth Platte, OP, that will include some of her poems (see About the Editors at the end of this volume).

I echo Art's thanks to many peace activists for this extraordinary group effort. I also thank Anna Lawton, professor emerita of

Georgetown University, who founded New Academia Publishing, and Grace Cavalieri, a past Maryland poet laureate and host of the Library of Congress radio series "The Poet and the Poem," for creating such a lovely publishing venue. Additional thanks to everyone at the current iteration of Anne Montgomery House (Diane Roche RSCJ, Clare Pratt RSCJ, Louise Lears SC, and their many young activists) for walking with me as I supported Art on this journey. Paul Magno and Kathy Kelly have consistently been there as knowledgeable readers and teachers. Blessings to Patrick O'Neill, who was honored with Sr. Montgomery and Paul Magno when all Plowshares activists received the War Resisters League peace award in 1986. (All three were in separate federal prisons at the time and received the award in writing through the mail.) Kathy Boylan took me to the Atlantic Life Community gatherings at Kirkridge twice, which provided essential context. Thank you to Blake Kremer, and to the many RSCJ who all provided essential background on Anne Montgomery. Negar Nahidian, a brilliant graphic artist, designed the cover.

A final note of deep gratitude directly to Art Laffin for seeking me out with this project. I'm so honored he did.

June 2024

Preface

Clare Pratt RSCJ
Former Superior General of the Religious of the Sacred Heart

Anne Montgomery, RSCJ, was a small, frail-looking Religious of the Sacred Heart determined to transform swords into plowshares, to bring peace to a polarized world. Her various nonviolent actions against nuclear weapons, her many sojourns in Iraq and Palestine with Christian Peacemaker Teams (now Community Peacemaker Teams), her participation in the walk to Guantanamo, came out of a life of deep contemplation.

She was an embodiment of the words in Paragraph 8 of her congregation's Constitutions: "The pierced Heart of Jesus opens our being to the depths of God and to the anguish of humankind."

The poems which follow came from the depths of her contemplative heart.

Anne Montgomery RSCJ

November 30, 1926-August 27, 2012

Daughter of Alfred Eugene and Alice Smith Montgomery, Anne was born on November 30, 1926 in San Diego, California. She once described herself and her older brother, Brooke, as "Navy brats" who knew both the East Coast and the West Coast very well, but not much in-between. Both her father, a rear admiral in the Pacific in World War II, and her mother, with a deep love of reading, gave their children a solid grounding in courage, faith, and respect for others. Anne's high school years were at Sacred Heart, Eden Hall, in Torresdale, Pennsylvania where, as early as the second year, she excelled as a writer. She then attended Manhattanville College of the Sacred Heart in New York City while her brother, two years older, was at the Naval Academy in Annapolis, Maryland, where she visited on special occasions.

Graduating from Manhattanville in May 1948, she entered the Society a few months later, having been accepted by Rev. Mother Gertrude Bodkin. One who was a novice with her remembers that Marie Louise Schroen named her "White Flame." She made her first vows on March 5, 1951. Her teaching ministry, which expanded to different fields over the decades, began on the east coast. Shortly after Anne went to Rome for the program of preparation for final vows known as probation, Brooke, now a Navy pilot, was killed in a Navy plane accident, a tragedy Anne carried with her over the years.

At the end of probation with Rev. Mother Zurstrassen, Anne was professed in Rome on July 30, 1956. She returned to the New York vicariate where she taught in Sacred Heart schools for several years. Her love of literature and poetry was evident, as was her ability as a teacher and mentor to other teachers, especially during her ten years at the Sacred Heart school on 91st Street in New York City.

In August 1970, Anne became a teacher at a street academy in Albany, New York, which served inner-city adolescents. It was here that she experienced firsthand the problems of the poor and people of color. In 1975, she returned to New York City to work with school dropouts in East Harlem, after a year's internship focused on children with learning disabilities. In both Albany and Harlem, Anne experienced the continuing problems of the poor and disenfranchised in our country as our domestic budget grew smaller for education, housing, and health care and the military budget expanded to develop more powerful nuclear bombs as well as a huge arsenal of newer military weapons.

Anne spent time at the Catholic Worker in New York City, living for ten years at houses of prayer, first at Covenant House of prayer and later with the Aletheia Community. She tutored at the Little Sisters of the Assumption, while joining with many others in protest of the nuclear arms race. She soon moved into a full-time ministry with peace activists, which was to continue for the next thirty some years on both coasts of the U.S. and far beyond.

In 1980, as a member of the Plowshares Eight which included Dan Berrigan, SJ and his brother, Phil, Anne took part in what was to be the first of several Plowshares disarmament actions in the coming years. Each action ended in arrest and indictment, trial, sentencing, time in either jail or prison followed by probation or parole. From the initial 1980 action, which occurred at the General Electric Plant in King of Prussia, Pennsylvania, all following Plowshares actions reflected the spirit found in Isaiah's words: "They shall beat their swords into plowshares and their spears into pruning hooks. And nations will not take up swords against nations, nor will they train for war anymore." (Isaiah 2:4)

Anne is likely the first RSCJ who ever had a suit filed against her in Federal District Court. It was titled, "United States v. Sister Anne Montgomery et al," and it followed another Plowshares action in 1985. She would probably not like that fact mentioned because she would consider it a distraction from the issue at hand: nonviolent actions to bring peace.

Anne never tired of explaining that peace actions must be based on continual community prayer, reflection, decision-making, and the prayerful consensus of the group in order to sustain those who had committed themselves to nonviolent civil disobedience and nuclear disarmament. She often commented that in her several times in jail or prison, she found that most women showed great care for her and others like her imprisoned with them. In addition, many were hungry for something spiritual and most understood the great disparity between the powerful and the poor and the effects this disparity had on American society. Quite often, Anne and other peace activists assisted women by starting prayer groups, Scripture study groups, and literature groups. Once out of jail or prison, she continued to teach and speak whenever she could about the danger of nuclear weapons in a world where peace was and is so fragile.

Anne's commitment to peace and nonviolence led her to go far beyond the United States. As a member of the Christian Peacemaker Teams (now called Community Peacemaker Teams, ed.), an ecumenical, non-violent anti-war group, Anne was in Iraq during the first Gulf War in 1991 and the following period of harsh economic sanctions against Iraq, which so affected the Iraqi people. In the next years, as a member of one of the CPT teams, she went to live in the Israeli-occupied West Bank where she spent several years and later in Hebron. Here she witnessed the ongoing and brutal conflict between the Israelis and Palestinians. During these years, Anne traveled back to Iraq at least twelve times, observing the terrible effects of war and standing with Iraqi citizens who had lost both family members and their homes. She witnessed the treatment of Iraqi detainees at the Abu Ghraib and other facilities. She walked with children and adolescents caught in the devastation of the bombings and the total disruption of their lives.

On one trip back to the United States, she participated in another Plowshares action, which again involved communal discernment and prayer, trespass on federal property, pouring blood of the group on the ground as a symbol of the cost of war, and sprinkling sunflower seeds as a sign of hope. This was done with her Baltimore, Maryland friends at Jonah House. For the past three or more decades her fulltime ministry of presence and work for peace had the strong support of her superiors in the Society of the Sacred Heart of Jesus. While Anne was an educator both by word and example she clearly preferred to be simply a support to those who worked for peace, and those who were poor and needy.

Her final Plowshares action, the last of eight, and at age 83, was on November 2, 2009 with the Disarm Now Plowshares group at naval base Kitsap-Bangor, about 20 miles west of Seattle, Washington. This base is the Navy's west coast nuclear weapons storage depot for the Trident submarines and the more than 2000 nuclear warheads, each warhead 30 times more powerful than the Hiroshima bomb, weapons that are illegal under international, national, and humanitarian law. With four other long-time peace activists, two of them grandmothers and two Jesuit priests, she entered the base. The five were arrested and charged with trespass and cutting fences. The federal judge, allowing no evidence of the violations of international law and humanitarian law, found the five guilty of federal trespassing and damage of federal property.

The day before their sentencing, the peace community of Tacoma, Washington celebrated a liturgy of peace and blessed them. The next day, all five were sentenced to time in prison. Anne's time in jail two months, followed by four months of electronic monitoring in Tacoma, Washington. She was welcomed by Blake Kremer, a lawyer for Plowshares and longtime friend of Anne's family. Once back in Redwood City, California she had a year of supervised release living with her RSCJ community and volunteering at the local Catholic Worker.

During those months, Anne was diagnosed with cancer and after a few months of chemotherapy, chose to discontinue treatment and go on hospice care. She moved to our Oakwood Community in Atherton, California for the last two months of her life. There she was often visited by other peace activists, friends, and sisters, either by phone, in person, or by letters. Shortly before her death, Anne received the 2012 Courage of Conscience Award from the Peace Abbey in Sherborn, Massachusetts. The award read: "Your commitment to education and your extraordinary moral leadership in the Pacifist Movement have provided a noble vision for all humanity." Her quiet leadership in the Atlantic Life community and the Pacific Life community, both groups deeply committed to peace and nonviolent resistance to death-dealing nuclear weapons, extended over many years. Knowing and loving so many people deeply committed to the work for peace was a source of great hope and strength for her to her last days. She died peacefully with her sisters present on the morning of August 27, 2012.

Peace activist and peacemaker, fearless and calm, a woman of deep insight and gentle humor, Anne embraced the challenge of building peace and encouraging others to work for peace and to create communities committed to works of peace. Contemplative and a lover of the poor, Anne stood simply and strongly against that which harmed people and the earth regardless of the cost to herself.

Lightly edited biography from the Society of the Sacred Heart of Jesus, used with permission.

Remembering Sr. Anne Montgomery, A Doer of the Word!

Art Laffin

The life story of Anne Montgomery is truly a remarkable journey of faith. I first met Anne in New York City at a prayer vigil during the first United Nations Special Session on Disarmament in 1978. I was undertaking a fast in repentance for my complicity in the arms race, and a small group of us would periodically gather for a prayer vigil at the Isaiah Wall, across the street from the UN. I was living in Connecticut and, along with several others, helping to start a small Christian peace community in New Haven. Anne was working in East Harlem teaching adults at the time, and was becoming more involved with peacemaking efforts, including the newly formed Kairos peace community, of which she remained a vital core member. Over the years, when I visited New York City, I would often stay with Anne and the Alethia House of Prayer community in Washington Square. Anne was truly contemplative at heart. Joining with her, Sister Eileen Storey SC, and other community members for early morning prayer was a very important part of my own spiritual formation.

In 1980 Anne participated in the first Plowshares action known as the Plowshares Eight. This unprecedented peace witness at the General Electric plant in King of Prussia, Pennsylvania called for the abolition of nuclear weapons, and marked the beginning of a new series of actions in which nonviolent resisters sought to enact the biblical prophecy of literally beating swords into plowshares. During the last four decades, these peace and justice makers entered weapons facilities and military bases, and – using hammers, blood and other symbols – carried out a direct act of disarmament. There have been 100 such actions to date. Anne went on to do seven other plowshares actions, including two that I was also part of, and the last of which – the Disarm Now Plowshares – took place in 2009 when she was 83. She served over three years in prison for these actions.

As more people tried to understand Plowshares actions and the role of nonviolent resistance to bring about true disarmament, I approached Montgomery about collaborating on a book about the Plowshares actions and nonviolent resistance. She agreed, and together we co-edited *Swords into Plowshares: Nonviolent Direct Action for Disarmament* (Harper & Row, 1987). In 1996 we published an updated and expanded version with the same title. Working together on this project not only helped me appreciate her gifts as writer and editor, but also as one who had a profound understanding of the scriptural justification for faith-based nonviolent action.

Anne's commitment to standing with and for the victims led her to many war-torn areas. In January 1991 she was part of the Gulf Peace Team Camp on the Iraq/Saudi Arabia border calling upon the United States not to bomb Iraq. She would return to that country many more times. Anne was among those activists who held a month-long liquids-only fast in 2000 aimed at ending U.S. support for U.N. sanctions against Iraq. She later became a member of the Christian Peacemaker Teams (CPT, now Community Peacemaker Teams), serving in Iraq, the Balkans, the West Bank, and Hebron. Explaining her witness in the West Bank, Anne said in an interview, "We say we're on the side of the people who have the biggest guns pointed at them. In this case, we think the (Israeli) occupation is wrong. It's wrong to take people's land, to destroy their homes, which is what the Israeli military does. As long as this unjust occupation continues, there can't be peace."[1]

Anne was also deeply concerned about confronting the sin and crime of torture. In December 2005 she traveled to Cuba with a delegation of 24 Catholic Workers and other activists to participate in a 70-mile walk and four-day fast and vigil near Naval Station Guantanamo Bay to call for the closing of Guantanamo, an end to torture and indefinite detention, and justice for all the prisoners. I was also part of this delegation. One of my favorite images of her is, at the age of 79, leading our walk/pilgrimage from Santiago to Guantanamo. Upon returning to the US, those participating in this delegation formed Witness Against Torture which remains very active today.

Keenly aware that "Our struggle is not against flesh and blood but the principalities and powers of this world" (Ephesians 6:12), Anne provided compelling insights into how nonviolent resistance actions are really experiments in truth that should be seen as acts of "divine obedience," rather than civil disobedience. She wrote:

> Civil disobedience is traditionally the breaking of a civil law to obey a higher law, sometimes with the hope of changing the unjust civil law... But we should speak of such actions as divine obedience, rather than civil disobedience. The term 'disobedience' is not appropriate because any law that does not protect and enhance life is no real law. In particular, both divine and international law tell us that weapons of mass destruction are a crime against humanity and it is the duty of the ordinary citizen to actively oppose them. (*Swords into Plowshares*, 1)

Following the 2010 Disarm Now Plowshares trial conviction, for which she served two months in federal prison and was placed on house arrest, she lived with her community in Redwood City, California. From there, in a March 1, 2012 letter to friends describing her cancer she wrote:

> I have been on chemotherapy for cancer, and it seemed to be helping, but, last weekend I had breathing problems and tests showed a lung full of fluid and that continuing any chemo, etc. would not help. I have been blessed by so much support, personal, and medical, that I know I must share that in some way with all those across our world who lack so much and are near desperation, especially for their children.
>
> I also know that the Spirit prays at the heart of the universe and that creation is an ongoing journey of death and resurrection, however mysterious that process is. Because it is energized by Love, we can enter into it rather than count on our own weak efforts and vulnerabilities and worry about failures. When I made my final vows, our group was named, "Joy in the Faith," I am coming to believe that it must somehow be possible since it is promised in the Beatitudes and that those who have nothing show us the way.

I am constantly filled with gratitude to you all who have done the nitty-gritty work of peace and nonviolent action and invited me to join you. I hope to be able to do so in a new way.

As Phil Berrigan said in his last letter, that work must come from our own vulnerability.

Much love,

Anne

Despite her physical limitations, Anne remained very active during the last six months of her life. Whenever I spoke with her by phone she conveyed news of peace activities on the west coast, and was very interested to know of acts of witness taking place elsewhere. She was elated to hear about the Transform Now Plowshares action on July 28 of that year at the Y-12 nuclear weapons complex at Oak Ridge, Tennessee, and offered her heartfelt support. A week before she died she was given the 2012 Courage of Conscience Award from the Peace Abbey in Sherborn, Massachusetts.

Montgomery's life is a testament to the Gospel truth that love casts out fear and that with God all things are possible! Her unwavering commitment to nonviolence, accompanying and interceding for the victims, engaging in nonviolent resistance to systemic violence, and working with people from all over the world to create the beloved community will serve as a constant reminder of what it means to be a Gospel peacemaker. In an interview with Fr. John Dear published in the *National Catholic Reporter* on May 1, 2012, Montgomery spoke of her deep conviction that all believers need to take to heart:

I also have hope in knowing that God's power and God's nonviolence are stronger than violence and war. Love is stronger than evil, hate, fear or war. The opposite of love is fear, and the government tries to keep us in permanent fear. When we come together in love and struggle for peace, we are no longer afraid and we can change things. As we trust each other and God, our fear lessens. So we can't be afraid to do the right thing. Love is always stronger, and that gives me hope.[2]

On August 27, 2012, God called Sr. Anne Montgomery, RSCJ, 85, home to her eternal reward after a long struggle with cancer. All who knew her lost a very special friend. The church lost one of Jesus' most steadfast disciples and prophets. And the world has lost an extraordinary peacemaker.

Editor's Note – June 2024: Twelve years after Anne's death a war now engulfs the Holy Land. Anne worked with Palestinian and Israeli peacemakers to prevent such a colossal tragedy! No matter who the perpetrator is, Anne opposed and resisted all violence, killing and war. Since the October 7, 2023 horrific Hamas attack in Israel which claimed 1,200 lives, the Israeli government has waged a genocidal war in Gaza. The U.S. government has supplied military aid and weapons to Israel to carry out its bombardment and siege of Gaza, which has resulted (as of this writing) in over 37,000 deaths, including over 15,000 children, over 85,000 injured, over 17,000 orphans, the displacement of some two million Gazans, and a catastrophic humanitarian crisis resulting in widespread famine (approximation of numbers from the Gaza Health Ministry).

Additionally, Save the Children estimates over 20,000 Palestinian children have gone missing during Israel's war on Gaza, with thousands separated from relatives or buried under the rubble. Gaza is now rendered almost uninhabitable, with people lacking adequate sources of income and access to water, sanitation, health or education. In a provisional order issued on January 26, 2024, the International Court of Justice (ICJ) found it is "plausible" that Israel has committed acts that violate the Genocide Convention. The court said Israel must ensure "with immediate effect" that its forces not commit any of the acts prohibited by the convention (ICJ, Order of January 26, 2024).

With all the victims and those crushed under the rubble, with all those who are denied the status of persons, I hear Anne crying out with many worldwide for a permanent ceasefire, peace, accountability, release of all Palestinian and Israeli captives, and reparations. I hear her voice joined with all those in the Holy Land, the U.S. and globally calling for an end to the Israeli occupation of Palestine, for no more U.S. weapons to Israel to support the war and occupation, for self-determination for Palestinians, and for a just peace in Israel and Palestine.

On January 23, 2024, the Bulletin of the Atomic Scientists re-affirmed its 2023 decision to set the iconic Doomsday Clock to 90 seconds before midnight due to the existential threats of nuclear war, the climate crisis, nuclear weapons upgrades being made by the U.S., Russia, and China, worsening world tensions, the Ukraine war, and artificial intelligence. Today, I hear Anne's voice echoing the words of Dr. King: "The choice today is... either nonviolence or non-existence."[3] I hear Anne's voice joined with all those working for environmental, social and racial justice. And I hear her voice in the pleas of everyone throughout the world working for the aboli-tion of war and nuclear weapons, and calling on the U.S. and eight other nuclear nations to ratify the UN Treaty on the Prohibition of Nuclear Weapons, as 70 nations have already done.

Based on Art's "In Memoriam" remembrance of Anne that was published in the National Catholic Reporter on September 15, 2012.

Reflections

From the living members of the original
Plowshares Eight: Dean Hammer, Molly Rush, and
John Schuchardt,
from Rabbi Lynn Gottleib,
who knew Anne in Hebron, Palestine and
New York City, and
from Anna Brown, who was a member of the
Kairos Community with Anne.

Reflection from Dean Hammer

Dean Hammer has been a member of the Plowshares Eight and Griffiss Plowshares. He practices psychotherapy in Vermont, and teaches clinical psychology at Antioch University New England.

The gift of walking with Sr. Anne Montgomery is a pearl of great fortune. Her soulful presence continues as a source of guidance and consolation. Anne's life is a work of art and a living prayer. Her goodness and devotion to peace and justice shines as part of the eternal flame.

We entered the preparation for the Plowshares Eight process at the same time in June 1980. The bible study began at Jonah House six months prior. Anne spoke less than most of us. Her presence in the group process can be characterized by Jesus' observation of Nathaniel: "Here is a true Israelite (a person devoted to God). There is no guile in him." Anne's lack of pretense served as a ballast during the stormy waters of the Plowshares Eight experience. She remains my teacher of benevolence and equanimity.

Reflection from Molly Rush

Molly Rush is a co-founder of the Thomas Merton Center in Pittsburgh, Pennsylvania, where she lives. She and Carole Sargent adapted the following statement from the 1989 book Hammer of Justice: Molly Rush and the Plowshares Eight *(Pittsburgh Peace Institute, 1989).*

As a member of the original Plowshares Eight, one of my most vivid memories of Anne Montgomery is being handcuffed together with her when we were taken to the Berks County Jail. Anne taught me yoga while we were both incarcerated.

At our trial, Judge Salus didn't much care for the rest of us, but he showed deference to both Anne as a Catholic sister, and Daniel Berrigan as a Jesuit priest. Both of them decided to use this to our advantage. When we were called to present our defenses, they stood together with Dean Hammer and me. Instead of answering the judge, we four turned our backs to him while remaining mute. The judge called it "an act of arrogance and contempt," and further "disrespectful and disorderly," but he didn't do more, probably because of Anne and Dan. Instead, he just left us standing there during closing arguments. While we did, one juror began to weep.

The judge said he regretted having to sentence Anne Montgomery. "Of all the people that I met in the Plowshares Eight, your inner peace, your sincerity, your ladylike behavior, and your real conscience has struck me more than anybody associated in this very difficult trial. You are truly a person to be admired." I wrote in my book that "Anne was livid about Salus's praise... She didn't want to be called 'a lady' in that situation."[4]

Reflection from John Schuchardt

John wrote the following to Art Laffin in an email exchange regarding the 43rd anniversary of the Plowshares Eight action, in which John and Anne participated. John recalls the impact Anne's reflections from the Biblical Book of Wisdom had on him and the Plowshares Eight community. He is co-founder of the House of Peace in Ipswich, Massachusetts.

Thank you for recalling the day the Holy Spirit whispered gently to all of us.

I so vividly recall Sr. Anne reading to us all from the Book of Wisdom, a long passage which I have turned to again and again these past 43 years.

As Dan [Berrigan] so simply said, "we could not, not do it."

Truly, as [Thomas] Merton tells, "In the end, everything depends upon our human relationships."

Sophia/Wisdom/Holy Spirit was received into our communities, with earnest searching and prayers and friendships. What a tapestry, truly, the mysterious weaving of the destinies of all of us...

Our step of faith, daring witness, was fruitful, beyond our expectations, but surely in harmony with our hopes, "We Are Filled With Hope." Plowshares witness carried for four decades surely dwells in the invisible and eternal reality, as with Elmer, Phil, Dan, Carl, Anne and so many, many companions on The Way...[5]

Sr. Anne read to us from The Wisdom of Solomon, found in The Apocrypha. I'm not sure about her translation? But mine is *The New English Bible*, Chapter 7, Verses 24-30, beginning: "For wisdom moves more easily than motion itself, she pervades and permeates all things because she is so pure," through to ".... against wisdom no evil can prevail."

It seems to me this was Anne's credo, her heart of faith. In any event, read by her, in her gentle of all gentle voices, it made a lasting difference in my life.

That may have been the moment (my memory is not clear about this, but maybe just a beginning) when I awakened to the reality that the Triune God enfolds the feminine: Wisdom, Sophia, Holy Spirit...

Interesting how we never know how a simple reading may reverberate in the life of someone in circle for a lifetime.

Reflection from Rabbi Lynn Gottlieb

Rabbi Lynn Gottlieb wrote the following to Art Laffin in an email exchange. She recalls the impact Anne had on her and the Palestinian people. She created a mural dedicated to Anne in Hebron. She is co-founder of Interfaith Peace Builders with Rev. Doug Hostetter, a program of the Fellowship of Reconciliation which eventually became Eye Witness Palestine. She is one of the first ten women to serve as a rabbi in Jewish history and a practitioner of Shomeret Shalom Revolutionary Jewish Nonviolence. Please see www.rabbilynngottlieb.com.

I was blessed to cross paths with Anne Montgomery over many decades in her front-line work against all forms of US militarism, including in its support of Israeli Occupation. Anne was fearless in her activism and was fine being arrested after pouring her own blood on a nuclear submarine or chaining herself to a home under the threat of demolition in Hebron. Anne traveled with and provided her own narration of events over many cups of coffee in the oldest coffee shop in the ancient city of Hebron. She was a mentor in the art of civil disobedience whose love and fearlessness were a force more powerful.

I was invited to create mural projects in Nablus, Balata and Hebron at the invitation of several Palestinian women's organizations and through the support of Abraham's Path organizer George S. Rishmawi. In Hebron, local organizers wanted to honor Anne's bravery and solidarity in Palestine with the mural depiction of her act of resistance to home demolition when she delayed the demolition for five hours by chaining herself to the house.

Photo by Rabbi Lynn Gottlieb, September 2012

The writing on the mural states: "In Memory of Anne Montgomery—A Friend of Palestine—She Resisted Occupation with the Power of Love—1926-2012."

Reflection from Anna Brown

Anna J. Brown wrote the following to Art Laffin in an email exchange. She reflects on Anne's involvement with the Kairos Community in New York City, and the impact she had on her. Anna is a political science and social justice professor at Saint Peter's University, Jersey City, NJ, where she helped to found the Dr. Martin Luther King-Kairos Social Justice House and The Center for Undocumented Students. She has been a member of the Kairos Community for the past thirty years.

You would hardly know who she was. Dressed in modest clothing, saying little about herself, and slight in physical stature, one might need to learn elsewhere about the mighty works of Sr. Anne Montgomery, RSCJ. Those of us blessed to be members of the Kairos community with her did know and were the better for it. "Montgomery," as the dear Elmer Maas affectionately called her, was an anchor of the community, an elder who taught us to be prayerful, loving, and firm in our commitment to peacemaking and resistance. Anne moved through life with a shining soul and a piercing clarity; there was no wasting time on personal drama. There was no dwelling on past peace actions and Plowshares arrests because there was always so much suffering in the world, and we needed to attend to it, which Anne did faithfully and consistently.

When members of the Kairos community, including myself, joined Witness Against Torture in a seventy-five-mile walk and protest of US-sponsored torture and indefinite detention at the Guantanamo Bay detention camp in 2005, 79-year-old Anne was there. A few days before the trip to Cuba, she had just returned from her work with the Christian Peacemaker Teams (now Community Peacemaker Teams, ed.) in Palestine and Israel. When the current US-sponsored slaughter of the men, women, and children of Gaza tempts me to lapse into despair, I pray to Sister Anne, who has one message for me: "Gather yourself together and get to work."

Anne nurtured and cherished her friendships and her life in the community, whether it be that of her religious community, the Atlantic Life Community, or the Kairos community. Her gentle way of being with us, the small kindnesses she showered upon us, and her soaring spirit continue to move and speak to me in the present day: be attentive, be loving, be prayerful, and resist, resist, resist militarism so that all peoples of the world may live in peace and harmony.

About This Poetry

Art Laffin

Anne Montgomery, RSCJ, was a nonviolent witness in war zones in the Holy Land and Iraq. She endured years of imprisonment because of her involvement in Plowshares antinuclear resistance actions. Her poems, borne out of her study of scripture, are rooted in her love for accompanying the marginalized, and rich with her experience of religious life and community. These poems provide insights into what it means to be human and a faithful follower of Jesus. Where possible, an introduction to some of the poems is offered to help provide a context.

This collection serves as both a powerful spiritual anchor and a source of inspiration for all peace and justice-makers. Drawing on her experience as a religious, teacher, and peacemaker, Anne's poetry contains powerful scriptural insights that can sustain people's hope during these perilous times.

Prologue by Anne Montgomery, RSCJ
Facing the Darkness

"A voice from the dark called out,

   'The poets must give us
imagination of peace, to oust the intense, familiar

imagination of disaster. Peace, not only

the absence of war.'

                  But peace, like a poem,

is not there ahead of itself,

can't be imagined before it is made,

can't be known except

in the words of its making,

grammar of justice,

syntax of mutual aid." (Denise Levertov)[6]

Another poet, Daniel Berrigan, contrasts prose as "an instrument of efficiency: it belongs to the 'things which are seen.' Prose moves things, gives orders, is logical, serves for argument, settles conflicts or makes war… Poetry is unnecessary in the sense that God is unnecessary. Poetry is useless in the sense that God is useless. Which is to say, God and poetry are not part of the kingdom of necessity, of that world of law and order (lawlessness and disorder) and sin and war and greed we name 'the fall.'"

   In Genesis, God the poet created more than water and land with evolving life-forms, subject to scientific study. We are faced with chaos, tamed by the division between light and darkness, of land from sea, with a Spirit hovering over all as a constant presence in an ongoing struggle: "The light shone in darkness and the darkness could not extinguish the light."

When we, trusting in that Spirit, cut through the last fence at SWFPAC and stood before the tomb-like storage bunkers for Trident missiles, the dawn grew in the West: a gentle image of multiple colors, muted but strong in their promise of victory over darkness, of the spirit of vulnerable love over the threat of chaotic violence. Paradoxically, the blinding, glaring lights by each tomb themselves were a kind of darkness in their promise of an idolatrous and false security.

John's Gospel introduces Jesus as the Light of the World, over-coming a darkness which cannot comprehend his way of nonviolent love, of no compromise with the political or religious power-brokers of his time. In poetic metaphor and symbol he consistently spoke "the grammar of justice." But he spoke most clearly and dangerously by his life, offering, not immediate results, but a Way of fidelity to truth-speaking and love of both friends and enemies: "a syntax of mutual aid."

In our Plowshares community we tried to speak the language of pilgrimage, of the way being the goal. We carried the symbols of hammers, blood, and sunflower seeds: hammers to transform weapons of death to human products, seeds to plant new life, and blood to remember the victims of war. We tried to walk in the Way, too, not only during the hours on the base, but also in our communal prayers and discernment, in our willingness to plan carefully, but also to stumble and make mistakes, perhaps not achieve immediate results, but to be one with the Spirit, so that:

"peace, a presence,

an energy field more intense than war,

might pulse then,

stanza by stanza into the world,

each act of living

one of its words, each word

a vibration of light-facets

of the forming crystal."

Gospel Reflection Poems

Notes on the poem "Christ is Risen and He Walks"
Art Laffin

This poem is not dated and it is not known where Anne wrote
it. One thing is known: she truly believed in the risen Christ. She
sought, as her good friend Dan Berrigan put it, to "taste" and "test
the resurrection in our bones."[7] Her understanding of Resurrec-
tion, borne out of prayer, service and resistance, is reflected in her
invocation of how Jesus is present in our midst, in each fragile
moment.

Christ is Risen and He Walks

Christ is risen and he walks
   within walled space and time –
      each fragile moment
         flickering and hoping for the next to break
            through the glass and hold the hand
               of eternity.

Christ is risen and his word
   waits in all withinness
      welcoming each unsaid,
         uncertain, unfinal, unframed
            phrase, broken in the middle,
               but open to meaning.

Christ is risen and his presence
   grasps the fluid shifting matter
      of our being here at all
         to walk with it and rest his head
            nowhere – but everywhere, all over,
               under and over.

Christ is risen and his face

    comes and goes, but now I –

        don't know – I know –

            Galilee is history – but not they and we:

                women, friends – faithful, faithless – untombed,

                untimed.

Palm Sunday, 1969

We tore the branches from the trees and sang
    as though the streets could know no other sound,
and yet from every alley beggars called;
lost children sobbed their emptiness;
slaves screamed in pain,
and old men died
alone.

We danced the dust into a hovering cloud –
    the stones would cry out only later
in the echo of our fear that,
for comfort, not kingship but Godhead had come too near –
but not for comforting
the living lost
and dead.

You who enter every gate of love and pain,
    come back;
slide off the ass's back once more,
and, falling three times, clutch our passive dust –
breathe blood –
then, struggling,
rise again.

Notes on the poem "Brothers"
Carole Sargent

During Anne Montgomery's discernment to become a Catholic sister, the mother superior told her that they wanted her to experience life and at least earn a college degree. She chose to travel around Canada, sometimes taking the train between New York and the West Coast via a scenic Canadian route. Her brother, who was still in high school, supported her emotionally at this time. Later he enrolled in the U.S. Naval Academy with the goal of becoming a Navy pilot and serving in World War II. His name was Brooke, although his fellow pilots sometimes knew him by the nickname Monty.

Brooke and Anne absolutely loved and cared for each other. She'd share many stories about her brother with her friend and lawyer Blake Kremer, one after the other, remembering all the little adventures they had as kids growing up.[8] Once they lived in Coronado, California, near San Diego Bay. While her father went yet again to sea during World War II, she and Brooke had bought a little sail boat that you could also manually row so they could have some naval adventures themselves. It was in terrible shape and was always sinking, but nevertheless they would try to go out to sea in it together. It was Brooke's job to sail, and Anne's to bail as quickly as she could. They would spend whole afternoons sailing around like that, having the greatest adventures. They would fish off the side and bring the catch back to their mother, who would poach the fish to make beautiful meals.

When Anne Montgomery was dying, she had a selection of just a few pictures around her, next to her, on her bed. One of these was her brother Brooke, looking like a 1950s Hollywood movie star. He had chiseled, handsome features and a big, warm smile. The story behind that photo was the cause of great mirth in her family. Brooke had finally achieved his goal of becoming a naval pilot, but he was technically the class of 1946. Because of the buildup of the war in 1945 his class graduated early to join the action, but he was commissioned just as V-J Day was announced. Determined to at least see the Pacific theater that his father had known so well, about a week after the war ended he got permission to fly out and land on the deck of an American aircraft carrier in the Pacific. When he landed, however, he realized that he had made a terrible mistake. He was on a Japanese aircraft carrier!

Given that it was now peacetime, the captain of the carrier radioed his captain and said, "One of your pilots has mistakenly landed on our ship. What should I do?"

The American commander radioed back and said, "Don't let him go until he writes a poem."

He did this, and then was granted permission to fly back. As he landed on his carrier, he saw everyone standing at attention on deck in their dress whites. A band played. After all, he had made history. Brooke "Monty" Montgomery was the first pilot ever to actually land on a Japanese carrier, albeit after this whole, horrible war had ended, and the only one to return safely as well. The crew saluted him (surely at his merciless expense), the band performed, and as he stepped down the ladder from his plane in the uproar, someone snapped the smiling photo that Sister Anne had at her bedside when she lay dying. "He's got the best smile on his face," remembers Kremer. "It's embarrassed and humiliated and happy."

Anne Montgomery finished college at Manhattanville, the College of the Sacred Heart, and she was invited to join the RSCJ order in 1948, making her first profession in 1951. Then in 1956 she went to Rome to prepare for her final vows. Part of this involved a long silent retreat of more than a month, as we saw earlier in this book. It was during this retreat in early February that she was brought to a superior's office and told, "Your brother just died in an airplane crash." He had died on February 1, 1956. After this she was expected to return to that silence. She was in Italy, far from her family. "It was incredibly painful for her that she couldn't talk with her parents," Kremer said, "and that she couldn't be there to mourn her brother with other people who cared about him. That was a pain that she carried to the end of her life." He was 28 by then, and the crash happened when two fighter planes collided at 40,000 feet near Ventura, California during a target practice run. The cause was determined to be pilot error. The other young pilot survived.

It would be inaccurate to read this poem about brothers as *necessarily* being about Brooke Montgomery. It might not have been. But knowing about the tragedy does offer a sense of its possible valences for her.

Brothers

I dreamt I held a husk –

  but that was my brother;

    his hunger

 drained my soul

    to what ours is: a
longing.

Where he had walked I could not

 follow:

to drink the wine of wonder,

  to feast on fire –

but dance whirlpooled to stillness,

  and quenched its flames in darkness.

For what he – prodigal – had spent,

  I clutch to close the crevices of an empty house,

    the sterile farmer of furrows ruled on a fertile earth,

      blossoming the lambs I fence,

      bursting with grapes I grasp to crush,

        lest their joy unfold my fingers.

And so I find you in my house,

   called here by our father,

to steal and squander the very self I

 saved:

     a stranger, my soul's brother,

      prodigal of all I hold to profit heaven.

The calf is killed,

   fattened for the bride I could not love,

and my bones, shaken by the wind,

   rise with its whisper.

Through falling leaves and fallow vineyards I walk the world,

     a beggar,

    bound for a country far,

    and home to find my brother.

Andrew

People were always trying to

    see; running,

        climbing trees,

           lifting children high

              above the crowding,

and that day – as usual –

    they came to me.

I was always the go-between:

    first for Peter,

this time for Philip and his friends.

And then

    on that minute,

      that hour,

the world turned round,

    for the hour was now –

as it was that first time when

      He

    turned and said,

     "Come and see."

I have been coming ever since,

    but now – then – always

        He is the One

           coming,

           lifted up

              for all to see.

And I Lord?

    but

  you said

    "Follow me."

Zacchaeus

Curious or crazy,
　I climbed
and lay clinging,
　　caught in the clouds that cluttered
　　　the sky of any mind,
　　the leaves dancing, taunting with veined,
　　　hypnotic hands
　　　　the foolish fancy
　　　　　that I could see.

Dizzy to dreaming, my eyes are
　　drawn down to a world
whirled
　　　in madness,
　　its still center a tree,
　　　roots serpent-coiled and
tearing
　　　　a cave – dark to its core.
　Poised at the plunge,

I am caught by a cry:

Come down –

quickly come down –

I would stay with you today,

stoop to enter the door

of your flesh

Steep the way and narrow

between pride

and

passion,

fire and

water;

one must pass

alone

and so we go

together.

Mary

I brought her home with me –

    Wisdom –

and waited,

     patient at her door,

with the passion of those who wait

      empty,

my soul a mirror

    crystalled

in the waters of creation,

  spirit stirred until

     ripples,

crossing and splintering the image,

    made him seem like

      everyman –

    timeless yet

     coming daily,

  untouched but

    closed in the man-made temples

     of this world.

And now I understood

    that the outcasts

        and the prostitutes

            come first.

So I said:

    Behold me, bound,

        the servant of

            each one.

Mary of Magdala

Stillborn my spring,
  conceived in sin
      and sickened in the winter
        of my frosted heart.

I wait, watchful,
    in the doorways of my childhood
      sold to strangers –
    and learn to dread each
          footstep
            stopping.

Under each beating row of bulbs
        flashes my fear
        like a beacon,
    but the soiled bones barred
        over my prisoned self –
            broken –
        can dance to no man's song.

The noontime of my passion faded

  before my morning dawned,

    and I long

      for the cool of the day

      when shadows,

        like nightmares,

         fade,

  when he,

  who walked in the beginning

      with woman –

        unveiled

  –will rise

      to light my night

      with splendor.

He stands at my door

  and knocks,

  and my fingers,

    slippery with myrrh

      rumble to open.

John

The stones cried out
　　and cut
　my unshod feet,
　　　sharp as truth,
　　　　dissecting bone and marrow:
for other feet this land must walk –
　　　　barren –
　gentle as its sand, as hard to
　　　grasp.

I prophesied to scattered bones,
　　but no breath came,
　　　and,
　taunted by their babel,
　preached peace to funneled winds
　　blowing war,
　　　echoing confusion.

When will he still
　　our strident streets
　　to silence? –

a thunderclap unhurled,

  a voice unheard, to break

    the barrier of sound;

a bruised reed pierced to bits

  our song of joy.

When will Justice

    leap,

  a lightning through our clouds? –

truth rise troubled from its tomb

    become

  the mother-womb of earth,

  the dark mirror of its waters,

    kissed by peace

      give new birth?

But

  no light shines –

    our candles smothered in damp
baskets

      woven by our fear –

  no chariot descends to lift the

    burden of our hope.

And I –

    a torch held wavering

      in a broken stand,

        smouldering in doubt,

          the flame

    lit at a banked and faithful

      fire.

Beside the well

    a tree

bowing to the sacred spring

    of age-old youth,

yet heavy with the harvest

    of a sunset year.

Together we wait

      daily,

    not seeking even

to gather

    or drink,

yet this memoried well

    mirrors more than fluid features –

    an echo rippling into words –

Give me a drink

    that I may thirst.

Give me fruit

   that I may hunger –

I who have begged for magic serpents

   and found the fish he signed in my dust;

who have gathered scorpions, doubly barbed,

    where beneath the tangled branches of my loves

          lay eggs

     ripe for breaking into birth;

who breathed incantations over stoney hearts

   to find the bread laid

    in my opening hands

      transformed

      and throbbing.

Teach me to ask by your asking

   who are bread and living water

     changed to wine,

      wine to blood,

       both flowing

       until

there is only one open

    Yes

   to the asking.

The well is deep
   I have gazed
    muddied
   into the darkness
     of days
   drawn out like drafts unquenching
     my loves
  languishing here and
    listening
  to a clatter of divided tongues
    darting poison.

The well is deep
   dreams drop
    and lie
   petrified
   slime-secreted those deaths
     their ripples clutching fearful
      at the corners of my mind.

The well is deep
   my shallow cup could scrape
    but its froth
   dirtied by the dust

of day to day

   by the dancing of this noontime devil.

And now

   no bucket

   no cup

nothing empty but my soul

   drained to its dregs

     and those dried up

nothing empty but my sieved fingers

   grasping the loss of what my coinage

     could not buy.

And yet

   I stoop

    not to forget what manner of woman

     meets me surfaced there

    not to forget a face

     kissed by the sky.

I thirst to pour out

  what I would drain

    from this welled heart of the earth

      dug

and bubbling crimson in the sun

into skins

new-sewn

and breathing.

When the well is empty,

our jars drained

by every passerby

with parched eyes

and withered hand

stretched out,

our bread broken and scattered

along a way

fragmented

into yes and

no,

He yet stands always

at the gate –

the Lamb who was slain at the heart

of our city –

at the crossroads

of sunlight and shadow,

flesh and stone,

the wind funneled,

gentle,

into "Come,"

yes, become

in the wedding

of ashes and fire,

the void and light,

of stream and source,

breath and life

emptied,

Abba –

brim-filled,

Amen.

I could see only his feet

who called me from that straight crowd

standing –

my bags there unclutched,

my heart here

where heaven

opened wide to my hearing

as I plucked his word from the ground

of my soul.

And I rose rhythmic
 to the dance of the sun
  in that dawning of days
   of journeys westward
    to Light.

In that Sabbath rest,
 while creation waited
  I rose,
   new-made,
    to worship.

And all around dry bones fluttered
  like fallen leaves
 to whisper judgement and shame,
  while the Word waited
   still
  to be gathered.

Four hands have seized the
 corners of my coffined being,
  lifted toward the light – have shattered
   the roof, a shrouded sky
  to shower the sun like stars
   upon our broken soil.

And I, lowered on the mantle of the winds,
hands stretched to either sea,
lie at his feet who reaches
from earth to heaven.

With fingers new-fashioned, supple, strong,
I seek to grasp each hand,
but hesitate, heart pulled back –
to break again.

For one is clouded leprous white,
one wind-withered as a crippled branch,
the third unformed by earth or heaven,
the last lightning-riven while drops fall darkened
to a crimson sea.

And I clutch the cloak of prismed light,
stretched taut from pole to pole,
and beg to be bound again, to be led again
where I would not go.

Note to the poem "S.C.J.M."
Clare Pratt, RSCJ

The title of this poem is reminiscent of the letters Religious of the Sacred Heart used to put in the top left-hand corner of letters. They stand for "Sacred Hearts of Jesus and Mary" in French.

S.C.J.M.

Lord, when the temple veil is rent
And my heart breaks
Before You, crucified,
What secret sins shall shun the light
Concealed in clouded eyes?

Not through darkened skies
Can glory clothe
This mountain's withered side
Where Love has pitched in agony
The scaffold of His tent.

But, all blood spent,
When water flows, –
The tabernacle opened wide –
May my heart be healed by echoes
In a soldier's broken cries.

The tomb is open,
And sunlight streams
Into darkness,
Yet You were there,
Alone.

A tomb is full of dead men's bones

And things we hate to mention,

Yet Yours was fresh and clean,

A place wherein no man had yet

Been laid.

Yet surely You have known,

And we are not alone

In sepulchres whitened or besmirched

With grime, the stench of guilt

Within.

You descended, and what depths

Are there in the darkness where

Queer dreams are born,

Shattered only by the light

Of morn.

The tomb is open –

That rock like bread seized

In the Maker's hands

Reaching out to

Touch us.

Shall we be healed then,

In the sunlight-sharpened shadow

Of this stone,

And, turning, touch hands

At dawn?

Prison Poems

Notes to the poem "FROM ALDERSON: LENT, 1985"
Jackie Allen-Douçot
Clare Grady
February 2023

Jackie Allen-Douçot is a member of the Hartford Catholic Worker. She participated in the Griffiss Plowshares action (1983) and the Thames River Plowshares action with Sr. Anne Montgomery (1989).

Clare Grady is a member of the Ithaca Catholic Worker, and she is most recently a participant in the Kings Bay Plowshares 7 (2018) and other actions, including the Griffiss Plowshares. Both served time with Sr. Anne at Alderson Federal Prison.

*****

"The walk Anne describes is a loop that runs inside the perimeter fence at Alderson Penitentiary that we walked multiple times a day.

The view outside the fence is of the spectacular hills along the Greenbriar River. Anne's poem reflects three perspectives… the looking out to reflect on the beauty of God's creation, looking inside the fence at the prison structure with its microcosm of poor, broken-spirited, mentally ill, and addicted warehoused by society, and finally the looking within her own soul where she meets Jesus."

FROM ALDERSON: LENT, 1985

I walk the road,
   one mile, more or less,
up the hill to view
   Outside
these sun-tipped hills,
   mocking? hollowed to hold death?
   or are they cradles of spring's
     birth, echoing our longing?

and Inside:
   A distorted mirror of worldwide
     pain:
     hospital–
     razor-wired detention–
     drug unit–
then downhill to the valley of our
   ordinary,
   mind-numbing
   daily
   come and go.

and yet Inward

   to face another mirror – darkened –

     someone walking long ago

      in small space

       and time

      but made a difference –

       how?

The "how" our hope

   not big numbers

    big names

    big news

  but its very substance-self

    discounted

    forgotten

    discontinued

    lost and buried

   and, behold,

     alive:

the Oneness

–we can name the Name–

   good news for all,

     breathed deep

   into the soil of our

    here

      and

        now

Notes on the poem "Thoughts on Deterrence"
Art Laffin

Like other people of faith – past and present – who were imprisoned because they upheld God's law in resistance to human laws that sanction injustice and killing, Anne, too, was imprisoned. Her witness is part of a long biblical and nonviolent tradition of resistance. This poem is written from jail following her involvement in the Trident Nein Plowshares action. To declare our independence from nuclear weapons and a war-making empire, Anne, myself, and seven other friends entered the General Dynamics/Electric Boat Shipyard early in the morning on July 5, 1982, and hammered and poured blood on missile hatches of the USS Florida Trident nuclear submarine and Trident sonar equipment. Using spray paint, the USS Florida was renamed USS Auschwitz. On a sonar sphere, we hung a banner: "Trident A Holocaust – The Oven Without Walls."

This poem reads like a Gospel parable. "Dying to live, losing to find – the fallow season of creation." The fallacy of deterrence is laid bare. The process of radical transformation and restoration is unearthed. Nothing can hold back the seed as it gathers strength from broken soil. For "the seeds in the darkness of this rotting place, drink deep from hidden springs, turn upwards, and in that push towards light, resist."

Thoughts on Deterrence

(In Season and out of Season)

The leaves are past their turning,
   like the road that curves between the trees
      and stops,
     dead at this door,
     deterred perhaps
       but only from going back–
         denying or forgetting
           that it must lose its boundaries,
             all signs secure in shape and color,
       and tunnel deep.

And so the leaves,
    dropping now,
    their last clinging to color and form
      cut short by an arbitrary wind.
They fall–
   a platitudinous lesson for slow learners:
    all about dying to live,
      losing to find–
  the fallow season of creation
     when seeds, in the darkness of this rotting place,

gather strength from broken soil,

   drink deep from hidden springs,

turn upwards,

   and

in that push towards light,

   resist.

(Written in the Correctional Institution for Women, Niantic, Connecticut, Fall 1982)

War Zone Poems

Untitled

"A river rises in Eden to water the garden; beyond there it divides and becomes four branches." (Genesis 2:10)

By the waters of Babylon my heart weeps –

We are exiles, all, from Eden where the rivers rise,

    where you, Basra, were built on the place

        of that first spring,

    where the Potter grasped mud,

      breathed it living,

      fired in the kiln of trial

        our very human selves.

Basra, beaten back to mud,

    your bodies pressed down to primal dirt,

    your souls bowed down to earth,

      where is Basra?

Where is Babylon? – where Rome? – where Jerusalem, City of Peace? –

    and you, Bethlehem, the least?

Are there boundaries?

Must we breach the walls, like those dividing

      man and woman,

slave and free,

 chosen and rejected,

 friend and enemy –

walls first built in Babel, whose towers threatened earth and

sky?

Who is Cain, who Abel?

 when brother kills brother and the soil cries out again;

 where the plowshare lies broken,

  the earth breeds armies;

  and the Word is fractured into babel: pentagonese and

newspeak.

Babylon is everywhere,

 the place of exile where Kurds and Guatemalans camp on

mountains,

  our homeless in the streets.

Jerusalem, Washington, Baghdad,

 every city is fallen indeed,

 and we all are exiles,

  banned from the Eden of our wholeness

   by flaming swords,

 borne not by angels but by would-be gods.

But Bethlehem, too, is everywhere;

small as seed sacrificed and fallen,

she grows,

fed by living waters,

a vine with many branches,

her grapes crushed,

her wine poured out

into the river, clear as crystal,

the channel of our peace.

And we, the exiles, wake and watch,

until Gethsemani is Eden.

Solidarity with the Victims: Return Trip to Iraq

(Anne Montgomery RSCJ wrote this in the autumn of 1992)

In this year of remembrance, as we attempt to recognize very divergent visions of the conquest of the Americas, it is important to see it as but one in a series of imperial adventures, like the endless reflections in a house of mirrors, the house built by the old world order, now the new one.

We need to focus certain images, to hold them steady in the face of the ever shifting mind-and-heart-numbing media barrage. For me, the past 20 months have deepened some of these images to symbols of the intentions and choices, actions, and consequences of our current principalities and powers. It became yet clearer to me in my third journey to Iraq since January 1991, that, even in the midst of so much worldwide warfare and impoverishment. the Gulf War, perpetuated in the sanctions, stands as the crucial violent event of our time as the deliberate setting of a future pattern.

The nature of the war and its efforts have been analyzed by U.N. and independent teams: Bombing "surgically" designed to reduce a progressive – and therefore threatening – nation to a Third World economy and dependency; an embargo to continue that destabilizing and weakening process.

Violence is an old story, but the weapons are the product of our time: the fuel-air bomb – the poor person's nuclear weapon. Behind it, the threat of the real thing in the Gulf; the biological weapon of pinpoint bombing of electric, water, and sewage plants; the subversion of the U.N. through bribes and threats. All this points to a world order that small nations might understandably reject.

That is the reality reflected in the faces and questions of the people in the streets and hospitals of Baghdad and Mosul, in the refugee camps of Gaza, the villages of Upper Egypt. Last summer a doctor in Karbala spoke of burn cases: mishaps resulting from the unaccustomed use of kerosene stoves after the bombing of electrical power stations. This summer I held children at a burn clinic in a small Egyptian village – burned feet, burned hands, burned bodies too young to understand that our "way of life" has much to do with theirs; that their half-built houses, which could have had proper stoves, were "bombed," too, with the job opportunities in Iraq.

Fire smoldered in the eyes of young teens in Gaza, filled with frustration and a learned hatred, a need to throw stones, perhaps because that is what they have been offered instead of the bread of opportunity. Their parents echoed the question of the Iraqis: "Why are you punishing the people if Kuwait was the problem?" and "Why the selective enforcement of U.N resolutions?"

Other images suggest their Gospel opposites: wheat fields burned by American pilots, who, after bombing Mosul, could then make a cross in the sky: seeds of hatred sown so that Muslims in Egypt attack Christians – because Christians have killed Muslims in Iraq. Yet, in the Christian village of Karakush, the Dominican sisters daily handed out 4,000 loaves of bread (baked from grain "unfit for humans") to Christian and Muslim alike, to families who took refugees into their own homes until there were 40 to a room. And, back in Baghdad, young lay Dominicans had formed a community of the destitute, "holding all things in common," in a graveyard – the safest place available.

In a Mosul hospital, a Moslem farmer of 80 could only pray: "My heart is too full to speak," as the beads slipped through his fingers. His younger companion voiced another repeated theme: "You are a large country; we are a small one. Why have we been hurt? We are farmers, ordinary people; tell Americans we are like them." A woman specialist later echoed him and described the young especially as "put in a cage without food or water or dreams for the future." The psychological damage evident here, and in those who still heard "bombs" and saw "soldiers" or who could not speak at all, was a reminder of one of the most diabolical effects of terror and malnutrition: a generation of hurt children, many physically or mentally handicapped, all with grim memories, even the baby whose first word was not "abuna" but "bomb."

But there are other vivid memories pointing to the sources of hope: the children of Karakush crowded on old school benches in July heat, still eager to learn, singing to us; handicapped children in Baghdad, secure in the love of the Missionaries of Charity, learning to dance to their own music; the rebuilt Jumhuriya Bridge, a tribute to the energy and creativity of a people concerned about rebuilding the spirit of a city where once there were few thieves and fewer beggars.

Most impressive perhaps was the ever-present "Welcome," the offer of tea or even a free shoe-shine – that to Americans. This summer, even more than last, Iraqis seemed determined to make a distinction between "people" (them and us) and "governments" (the great powers that war on the innocent and their own government that does not share the suffering). Paradoxically, the sanctions and the sense of victimization have created a greater sense of unity and determination, even, as one cleric put it, "a new Iraqi personality": creative and hard-working where once everything could be bought from abroad.

But no amount of creativity can replace what *must* come from elsewhere: medicine for leukemia and diabetes, anesthesia, and on and on, to say nothing of milk for babies who die if they cannot be breastfed by undernourished and traumatized mothers. The frustration and anger of doctors were encapsulated in the words of one: "I would like to help Somalia." Iraq could do so if the embargo were lifted. How to live with a national disaster for which a simple answer is simply refused?

In our own sense of helplessness, we can at least "watch," refuse to flee awareness, pray to maintain faith in the Way of nonviolence, and actively resist the powers. They do not grasp the weapons of love, of forgiveness, the refusal to hate enemies, or to place an embargo on the human spirit. Jesus did more than build bridges; he literally took the place of the enemy, the one scapegoated. One Iraqi painting shows two faces: an Iraqi and a U.S. soldier, with the words "I Am You."

Finally, the story of Jonah becomes a symbol for our own inner conflict as a rebellious people unable to accept God the Merciful, that in asking pardon we might receive the power to forgive ourselves and others. We need to risk repentance, admit, "I know it is my fault that this great storm has come upon you." (Jonah 1:12) We must allow ourselves to be thrown into the depths of the sea, the belly of the whale to rise again to the surface of the reality we have plumbed, one with ourselves and our sisters and brother. And then we must walk from end to end of our imperial city, ourselves clothed in the sackcloth of self-knowledge, one with the "enemy." "I Am You."

PSALTER:

THE SECOND WATCH

The heavens declared the glory of God;
    the sun stepped forth from its tent of clouds
        where light and darkness, wed at night,
            gave birth once more
              to hope.

And silver wings across the dawn
    or banked, silent, against the crimson sunset
   seemed as graceful as home-bound geese,
        until we remembered when,
         in the moon's darkness,
          we first woke to the sound of bombers.

Each evening they return, the mighty nations,
    and prowl the darkness;
they snarl like dogs across the sky;
they howl for their prey:
        the city,
        its children,
        their mothers.

Have pity, O God, have pity,

  for in the shadow of your wings

    we gather them for refuge

      and till harm pass by,

      and till the hounds of death run to their kennel,

        wave upon wave.

Awake, O my soul, watch and pray,

      remember;

Ours is the desert

  but theirs is the city of death.

Watch with the watchman;

  dream of the garden;

  and awake the dawn of his rising.

Then shall we not fear the terror of the night,

  nor the missile that flies by day,

    God's pinions our cover,

      our only shelter

     trust in the Almighty.

When faithfulness looks up from the earth

  and justice down from the heavens,

    God proclaims Peace:

      The Merciful

      The Advocate

      The Restorer.

Resistance/Witness Poems

Introduction to the poem "Impressions from the Prophets or G.E. Re-entered"
Art Laffin

I met Anne in the spring of 1978 in New York City at a Fast for Disarmament that I was involved in during the first United Nations Special Session on Disarmament. There was a vigil at the Isaiah Wall across the street from the UN and Anne joined our small witness. I was immediately taken by her gentle prayerful spirit and her deep-held commitment to justice and Gospel nonviolence. For Anne, reading the prophets and praying over their words meant following their example! She deeply understood that the call of Isaiah and Micah to beat swords into plowshares was not a nice idea for theologians and others to theorize and write about, but a divine mandate to be lived! Thus, I was not surprised when I first learned that she joined with seven other peacemakers to carry out the first Plowshares action at the General Electric nuclear weapons plant in King of Prussia, Pennsylvania on September 9, 1980. This poem, written from jail soon after her action, speaks of the biblical tradition and vision which compelled her and the others to act: *Thy will be done on this earth, your earth, our earth.*

Her concluding lines of the poem speak of the hope and promise that awaits those who place their trust in God: "In waiting and calm shall we now be; in quiet and trust lies our strength; our way committed to the Lord, our trust in his action. He will make justice dawn like the light, bright as the noonday sun, the vindication of the little ones who possess the earth."

Impressions from the Prophets
or G.E. Re-entered

September 20, 1980

Voices, like footsteps that come and go

     and, beyond,

  the echo of the morning star, robed in darkness:

    "This is the way; walk in it –

    Turn not to right nor to left."

The sword is drawn

    (or is it a missile?)

arrowed from a bow bent

    to bring down the oppressed and the poor.

But you, Lord, set our feet on the way,

    in the dawn of your coming,

      a judgment as certain

        as the light of day.

Unclean the idols,

    metal-plated, gold-bright images of death,

      triple-horned blasphemies,

     no breath of life in them,

Woe to those who say, "Awake,"

    to dumb shapes, "Arise,"

       for their own words shall destroy them,

         their own counsels devour them,

      because of the violence done to the land,

       to the cities and to all who dwell in them.

Of what avail is the molten image and lying oracle

     that its very maker should trust in it?

But the Lord is in his holy temple;

    silence before him, all the earth!

His word comes forth

   like the ringing of bells,

    the sounding of gongs,

  hammer on anvil

    swords into plowshares,

    stony hearts melted

       to flesh

        turned like the sod of a fresh-furrowed earth

         to breathe new life.

The warm circuit of hand clasping hand,

    life-blood shared

      like that spattered in this metallic temple

this place of human sacrifice

    shattered —

But our circle —

    a world made one

    a song in unison:

        "Forgive us, as we turn, sisters and brothers;

      Thy will be done

           on this earth

              your earth,

            our earth,

           as sacred as heaven."

Around us faces white as the dried bones

        of the already dead

      (Will the Spirit breathe in them?)

They say to us: "Have no visions.

      Do not cry out for us

        what is right;

speak flatteries to us, conjure up illusions.

      Out of the way! Out of our path!

        Let us hear no more

          of the Holy One of Israel."

But he who is God and not man

    the Holy One present,

        will not let the flames consume us.

In waiting and calm shall we now be;

    in quiet and trust lies our strength;

    our way committed to the Lord,

        our trust in his action.

He will make justice dawn like the light,

    bright as the noonday sun the vindication

        of the little ones

           who possess the earth.

Introduction to the poem "Sea Trials"
Art Laffin

The context of this poem is centered around the first sea trials of the Trident nuclear submarine, the USS Ohio, which was built at the General Dynamics/Electric Boat (EB) Shipyard in Groton, Connecticut. This event occurred at sunrise on June 17, 1981, which is also the Feast of Corpus Christi in the Catholic Church. Anne and I were among the 50 people, two of whom were arrested as they swam to stop the trial, who held a nonviolent witness on the banks of the Thames River in Groton to decry this nuclear sin. This poem reflects the horror of this sea trial of the nation's first of eighteen Trident nuclear submarines to be built, what the Pentagon defines as the "ultimate first strike weapon," the colossal peril it portends for the human family and all of creation, and the moral necessity to resist. As Anne writes: "We cling to our battered earth, tossed by terror… And so we cast our words, as fragile as wheat, on the water–our bread broken and shared–spirit–life–sown on earth sown on water–and the day rises."

Two months earlier, on April 25, 1981, EB and the Navy launched a fast attack hunter-killer nuclear submarine named the USS Corpus Christi. The use of the name "Body of Christ" for this nuclear submarine prompted a national uproar in the faith community, and there was a large resistance action when the submarine was launched. The Navy later renamed the sub the USS City of Corpus Christi. Mitch Snyder, an activist from the Community for Creative Nonviolence in Washington, DC, also conducted a long fast to decry the use of this name for this weapon of mass destruction.

Sea Trials

Feast of Corpus Christi, 1981

This is the night of sowing

    bannered words, wind-blown

        and fallen on these rocks

          hard above the river.

And, in the dark that holds back the dawn,

    a demon seed is planted in that sacred stream

        we can almost touch –

          living –

    while grey wings, hovering,

        innocent as Eden,

    await the transformation of light.

The wind is rising –

    as once in Galilee –

  and we cling to our battered earth,

      tossed by terror,

    lest it turn to molten stone

      under the dark shadow

        of a hungry god passing.

Yet light dawns, re-members us,

    re-minds –

  Behold those born on air, on water:

    the gulls – the swan –

   who rest on the word that calls us:

    "It is I: do not be afraid,"

     even now.

And so we cast our words,

  as fragile as wheat,

  on the water –

 our bread broken

  and shared –

  spirit – life –

   sown on earth,

   sown on water –

and the day rises.

Introduction to the poem "Feast of the Innocents: 1991"
Art Laffin

In an effort to destroy the newborn Jesus, King Herod ordered the execution of all the boys in Bethlehem and surrounding area who were two years old or less. A voice was heard in Ramah –Rachel weeping for her children… because they are no more! (Matthew 2:18) The Catholic church marks this unspeakable slaughter with a special feast day on December 28 named for these murdered Holy Innocents. The massacre of the innocents has continued throughout history and up to the present.

This poem is borne of lived experience. Anne heard the voice of Rachel – past and present – and acted! In her peace witness in war zones, Anne witnessed firsthand the suffering, death and destruction caused by modern Herods, most especially in Iraq and in the land called "Holy." She not only stood with victims and those crying out for justice in these zones and living under occupation, but also nonviolently resisted imperial death-dealing decrees ordered by today's Herods at the Pentagon, White House, weapons facilities and elsewhere. We, who are members of the Atlantic Life Community, the extended faith-based and nonviolent resistance community of which Anne was an integral part, now read this poem during each annual December 28 Holy Innocents commemoration witness at the Pentagon. To prevent such massacres from continuing we strive, as Anne did, to follow the nonviolent example of the crucified and risen Jesus, to remember the victims, to resist all injustice and killing and to witness in hope for a new humanity.

Feast of the Innocents: 1991
In Memoriam: Mass Graves

Anne Montgomery RSCJ

A voice in Ramah – a voice in Panama, Iraq–

weeping,

as yet again, Herod proclaims new birth

a threat,

the young expendable,

beginnings buried:

bulldozed into ditches,

shoveled into unmarked graves,

cast into the sea,

or flamed to ashes.

But in the sand and sea,

grass and cinders,

in silences,

the question will not die:

"Where is the one who is born?"

the child who sees with one eye –

or not at all,

who walks with one leg –

or never again,

whose dreams were shattered by shrapnel,

hunger stilled by pain.

The year's death reminds us of an old story,

a nightmare that will not go away,

but, dragon-like, rises from the sea,

blinds the dawn,

blasphemes God's name and dwelling

with fire from heaven

on those, uncounted, who do not count:

"You, the nameless, do not exist."

So it has been decreed,

for to allow the naming,

to confess reality and promise,

means new birth,

new time,

new humanity.

And so on this hill, clothed by the year's new grass,

the Child gives each of you whom no one can name

or even number,

a new name – beyond our comprehension –

and to us who gather here, a hope, a challenge,

a new way back to an old land.

It is for those with a journey to make,

and on it the redeemed will walk.

They will meet with joy and gladness,

sorrow and mourning will flee. (Isaiah 35: 9-10)

Feast of the Innocents

We, the Magi – the foolish folk

following stars,

journeyed light-years

in moments

and found

there is no going back

by the same road

to those fenced-out,

walled-in

worlds apart.

Here at the court of Herod,

this burnt-out mockery of a fallen star,

we stand

to close our circle,

the cycle of the year

when mother woke to weep

on trampled seed,

cradled now in mud huts and prison cells,

in shallow trench or river bed,

while shrouded death

crouched in silos.

Here we brought our gifts, ourselves,

    hoping that,

        like seeds sown on this frozen ground,

          they might burst:

            ashes to flame

              or flowers,

            stones to flesh,

            the wine of our blood

              to dancing, –

And found –

    ourselves the seeds,

        fallen,

         broken,

        empty –

in the desert of our flight

    to freedom,

    as pure as truth,

      a Child.

Miscellany Poems

The Deer

Etched innocence, then beauty bounding,

Is this joy, in moment caught,

One before the Fall created,

Or sweetness by Love–priceless bought?

Wonder poised to answer wonder,
Flight from sight but not from mind,

What answer to a world of darkness

In this vision will I find?

Wisdom shaping to Your Image,
Love fire-forging, undefiled,

Is this Your Word in silence speaking

To the senses of a child?

Is not all creation Christed,
Anointed by the Spirit's breath?

Reflecting light from Face in glory,

Matter mirrors life, not death.

Clay in His hands yet can sight give;
Him what pain this joy did cost:

Not blind to see my Christ then;

May this vision not be lost.

"…while it was still dark, Mary of Magdala came to the tomb. She
saw that the stone had been moved away from the entrance …"
(John 20:1)

Empty tombs, like open doors,
    are signs of hope;
the very emptiness, creating space,
  reminds us of the false ways
    we build walls,
      set limits,
    are turned back by stones of fear
     each passing through a little death
       would move,
       roll back
     to reveal the infinite
      flowing, emptying, filling
       freedom to be.

Only at such moments can hope,
    reborn –
  a spring released from the heart of the earth –
    burst forth,
      push back concrete slabs,
      flush out silos:
       those new tombs of poisoned eggs –

Hope –

    a spring released

        to heal our dug and broken earth.

"The man's sight began to come back…" (Mark 8:24-25)

I have seen walking with willow wands,

      touching magic as they pass,

          the trees,

and our earth groans at their uprooting,

      torn and trembled

        by this new birth

    of light

      searing my seeing to cinders.

But the cool hands of earth

      bank my fire to flame again –

        to focus first

          on a face.

And so – dark –

      my self mirrors clear one self

         in shifting patterns filtered to form features

            dancing on the walls of my world,

               shapes reshaped

                 until

Through spectrumed layers of

    shade and shadow

I walk a moon-path through this echo-land,

    its mist-walls melted,

    to my mirrored self –

    the visioned word unframed and formless

      sounding out

      a world

      transformed by splendor

      circling free and

      centered

      on this sun.

Introduction to "Prayer at this Kairos Time"
Art Laffin

This undated prayer by Anne is as relevant now as when she wrote it. A dictionary definition for Kairos is: the Greek word for "an opportune or decisive moment." A biblical understanding of "Kairos" means: "the appointed time in the purpose of God, the time when God acts."

These two Kairos documents from South African and Palestinian Christians expound on the meaning of "Kairos" in light of their respective nonviolent struggles for justice and liberation. In "The Kairos Document: Challenge to the Church of S. Africa, 1985," South African Christians, calling for an end to apartheid, wrote: "This is the Kairos moment of grace and opportunity, the favorable time in which God issues a challenge to decisive action." See "The South Africa Kairos Document 1985," at the Kairos Southern Africa website (kairossouthernafrica.wordpress.com).

The Kairos Palestine document titled: "A moment of truth: A word of faith, hope, and love from the heart of Palestinian suffering," was issued on December 11, 2009 by a group of Palestinian Christians calling for an end to the occupation of Palestine by Israel. See the Kairos document "A moment of truth: A word of faith, hope and love from the heart of Palestinian suffering," at the Kairos Palestine website (kairospalestine.ps).

Prayer at this Kairos Time

In this Kairos time of crisis and challenge, may we, like Mary of Nazareth, be open to the Spirit who calls us to new ways of incarnating the Word of truth and love.

In the face of harsh judgment even by those closest, may we, too, ponder deep in our hearts a response inspired by the nonviolent Christ who went beyond traditional teachings to grow to maturity in wisdom and grace.

May we invite the servants in the house of our Church to respond in trust to the faith that turns water into new wine, bursting the old skins of paternalism and outgrown legalistic structures.

May we, in the bold meekness of the Syrophoenician woman, challenge our Church to an inclusivity that dissolves fear to enrich and fill up the Body of Christ.

May we, by nonviolent and creative actions that speak louder than words, pour out whatever gifts we have, remembering the promise to the woman at Bethany: "Wherever the gospel is preached throughout the world, what she has done will be told in memory of her." (Mark 14:9)

May we have the courage to leave our securities and publicly follow the way of the cross to stand by the One who rejected the sword, healed the enemy, and challenged the perversion of truth by fidelity to it.

May we stand firm, even when darkness and chaos seem to fill our threatened earth, and express hope in the hidden energy of creative hope and love.

May we carry the message to the fearful disciples of the resurrection of a new humanity, birthed by the Spirit in the heart of a creation that groans " in the pains of childbirth right up to the present time." (Romans 8:22)

Introduction to "Declaration of Conscience"

The following is the statement from the Pershing Plowshares who carried out a plowshares action at the Martin Marietta weapons plant in Orlando, Florida on Easter Sunday in 1984. Group member Patrick O'Neill, who said that Sr. Anne wrote it, notes that, "This statement awed me in 1984 and still does 40 years later. Anne was at One with the God of Love and Peace Our action was Easter, Passover & Earth Day!"

Declaration of Conscience
April 22, 1984 (Easter Sunday)

In a time of the militarization of thought, of oppressive silences and twisted words that call the Pershing—offensive in speed, range, accuracy—a "defensive" weapon, we decry these realities; we express our desire to repent of the deeper violence that "secures" power and property while it bankrupts the spirit of a nation pledged to a welcome for the world's oppressed and to life, liberty and happiness for all. We act as a prayer that our hearing and vision be healed, that those we call "foreigner" and the invisible poor of our world may be seen, recognized and named our sisters and brothers, that we be led out of the darkness of despair and apathy into the light of hope.

We act in hope that this Passover may be a new liberation from the consumer lifestyle that enslaves us; from the fear and false securities that paralyze us; in the conviction that, in the midst of multiplied and impotent words, we must risk our bodies to conquer despair. We hope that, in a vulnerability open to the power of God, we can be healed of our violence and, empowered by love, break through the walls that divided "friend" from "enemy."

We act in love, in this Easter, this "dawn" of new life: responsible love—recognizing our relationship to these weapons which we must transform, to their creators, all of us in our shared violence and apathy, to their victims who cannot act; communal love—conspiring, breathing together, that we may be one, East and West, North and South in a more human and faithful world; obedient love—enfleshing the prophets' command, "They shall beat their swords into plow-shares and their spears into pruning hooks; one nation shall not raise the sword against another, nor shall they train for war again."

In choosing to disarm our own fear and to say NO to one weapon at its source, we celebrate the renewal of life; we choose the way of love that we and our children may live.

About the Editors

Lead editor Art Laffin coedited with Anne Montgomery two editions of *Swords Into Plowshares: Nonviolent Direct Action for Disarmament* (Harper & Row, 1987; Fortkamp Publishing-Rose Hill Books 1996; Wipf and Stock Publishers, 2010), and is editor of *Swords Into Plowshares: A Chronology of Plowshares Disarmament Actions* 1980-2003 (Wipf and Stock Publishers, 2010). For a chronology of Plowshares actions from 2003-2018 see "A History of the Plowshares Movement: A Talk by Art Laffin," *The Nuclear Resister,* October 22, 2019.

He is also the author of a new edition of *The Risk of the Cross: Living Gospel Nonviolence in the Nuclear Age* (Twenty-Third Publications, 2020). A member of the Dorothy Day Catholic Worker in Washington, D.C., he has long been active in the faith-based nonviolent movement for peace and social justice.

Assistant editor Carole Fungaroli Sargent is an RSCJ Associate. She helped the RSCJ open the welcoming community Anne Montgomery House in Washington, DC, and she co-directed it during its first year. Sargent publishes about Roman Catholic sisters, especially those active in nuclear disarmament. She is the author of *Transform Now Plowshares: Megan Rice, Gregory Boertje-Obed, and Michael Walli* (Liturgical Press, 2022), and two previous books for Farrar, Straus & Giroux. With Jesuit Fr. Drew Christiansen SJ, she co-edited the award-winning *A World Free from Nuclear Weapons: The Vatican Conference on Disarmament* (2020) and *Forbidden: Receiving Pope Francis's Condemnation of Nuclear Weapons* (2023), both from Georgetown University Press. From 2019-2023 she guided Sister Jeanne Clark OP to publish an award-winning book with editor Robert Ellsberg including some of her poems: *All the Way In: A Story of Activism, Incarceration, and Organic Farming* (Orbis 2023), and Sargent produced the audiobook. She is writing a biography of Sr. Ardeth Platte, OP, and it will feature poems by Carol Gilbert OP. She is founding Director of the Office of Scholarly Publications at Georgetown University.

Graphic designer Negar Nahidian teaches at Georgetown University. She is also a peace activist who has gone to Congress with CODEPINK and Teachers Against Genocide. Her work incorporates classical Persian motifs and calligraphy with modern design and technique, weaving together the aesthetics of East and West.

Notes

1   Art Laffin, "In Memoriam: Anne Montgomery, A Doer of the Word!" *National Catholic Reporter*, September 15, 2012, also published in *The Nuclear Resister*, August 28, 2012.

2   John Dear, "'Violence ends where love begins': A conversation with Sr. Anne Montgomery," *National Catholic Reporter*, May 1, 2012.

3   Martin Luther King, Jr., "Pilgrimage to Nonviolence," *The Christian Century*, April 13, 1960.

4   Carole Sargent worked with Molly Rush on this statement based on a book about her, Liane Ellison Norman, *Hammer of Justice: Molly Rush and the Plowshares Eight* (Pittsburgh Peace Institute, 1989, pages 33, 40, 168).

5   Elmer Maas, Phil Berrigan, Dan Berrigan, Carl Kabat, and Anne Montgomery.

6   "Making Peace," by Denise Levertov, from BREATHING THE WATER, copyright ©1987 by Denise Levertov. Reprinted by permission of New Directions Publishing.

7   Daniel Berrigan, SJ, "To Dwell in Peace: Unitarian Universalist Peace Fellowship Lecture," Given at the General Assembly of the Unitarian Universalists Association of Congregations, 1999. Republished as "An Ethic of Resurrection," in *Testimony: The Word Made Fresh* (Maryknoll, NY: Orbis Books, 2004), 225.

8   Blake Kremer, interview with Carole Sargent, December 29, 2017. Most facts in this section came from that interview. It was originally part of Chapter Four, "To Know Megan Rice, Meet Anne Montgomery," in *Transform Now Plowshares: Megan Rice, Gregory Boertje-Obed, and Michael Walli* (Liturgical Press 2022), but Sargent edited it out for length. It works perfectly here.